This book belongs to:

....

Using This Book

- Use the scenarios in this book as starting points for discussions with your child. Ask them to find the picture stickers and answer the questions.

- Encourage them to use the wipe-clean Happiness Diary wallchart to record their feelings. Try setting aside some time with your child at the end of the day for them to consider and talk about the questions on it. They can use the feelings stickers or draw in a face to show how they have mostly felt that day.

- Recording their feelings should be their choice – it doesn't matter if there are days when your child does not want to complete their Happiness Diary.

- Remember to always praise their efforts and perseverance, even if they do not wholly succeed. This helps to build a growth mindset and encourages them to keep trying.

- Being able to recognise and discuss their emotions will help them to be more aware of their well-being. The techniques explored in the book will show them a variety of ways to boost their mood when they feel down or anxious.

- Using the Happiness Diary can help your child to understand that, though they may not be able to control what happens in their daily lives, they can manage their reactions. With regular practice and use of the techniques that best suit them, your child can develop a positive attitude, maintain a calmer outlook, learn to avoid conflict, and ensure a greater feeling of happiness.

ISBN 978-1-78270-404-1

Copyright © Award Publications Limited

All rights reserved. No part of this publication may be reproduced or utilised in any form or by any means electronic or mechanical, including photocopying, recording, or by any information storage and retrieval system now known or hereafter invented, without the prior written permission of the publisher.

Published by Award Publications Limited,
The Old Riding School, Welbeck,
Worksop, S80 3LR

/awardpublications @award.books
www.awardpublications.co.uk

24-1141 3

Printed in China

The Children's Book of HAPPINESS

Sophie Giles
Illustrated by Chantal Kees and Angela Hewitt

AWARD PUBLICATIONS LIMITED

Lonely Together

Everyone in Noah's family is always so busy. Noah usually plays alone and often eats his dinner in front of the television.

He'd really like to tell everyone about his exciting day at school, but there never seems to be a good time.
Why is Noah feeling sad?

Sharing Time

Now, after their busy days, Noah's family all sit together to eat and talk about what they've been doing. They all help to tidy up, so sometimes there's time to play a game too. Everyone enjoys this special time together.
Do you have family time?

I enjoy family time together

Sensory Overload

Lucy is looking forward to a special trip to the museum with her grandad, but when they arrive in the city, she is overwhelmed by the crowds and busy streets, the noise and all the new things to see. Lucy begins to cry.
Why is Lucy upset?

Calm Concentration

They stop for a moment and Grandad gives Lucy a fruity sweet and asks her to describe the flavour. Lucy closes her eyes and concentrates on the taste, blocking out the busy city. Soon she feels calmer and they carry on to the museum.
Can you focus to calm yourself?

I focus to keep calm

Shopping Sadness

It's Saturday and Oscar wants to go to the shops to spend his pocket money. After a long day at the mall with Mum, he finally chooses a new toy. But after he's played with it for a short time, he is soon bored.

Why do you think Oscar might feel unhappy?

Nature Nurture

Oscar asks Mum if they can go to the forest park with his friend. They spend the day exploring, paddle in a stream, have a picnic and build a den.
They have a great day and make lots of fun memories.
Do you boost your happiness in nature?

Being outdoors makes me happy

Static Slump

Meena has spent hours watching TV and playing on her games console. Normally she enjoys doing this, but now she feels fed up and grumpy and doesn't know why. She flops onto the sofa with a big sigh. **Why do you think Meena feels the way she does?**

Mood-Boosting Movement

Meena realises she has been sitting down for ages. She decides to try a dance game instead and invites her brother to play too. They love trying to match the moves. It's great fun and Meena feels happier. **What sorts of activities improve your mood?**

I enjoy being active

 **Jealous of Others**

Lily's friend Olivia has a great voice and is going to sing the solo in the school musical. Her other friend Shauna has been picked to star in her ballet school's show. Lily doesn't like singing or dancing. She feels left out and really glum.
Why does Lily feel this way?

Focus on Your Own Strengths

Lily is happy for her friends. She can't do what they do, but she focuses instead on the things she enjoys. She even enters a science competition where she gets to meet one of her favourite scientists.
Can you focus on your own strengths?

Whirling Worries

Ned can't sleep. His mind is spinning. He's worried about the homework he hasn't finished, an argument with his best friend and whether he'll make the team on Friday. He can't calm his thoughts to get to sleep. **Can Ned do anything to help solve these worries now?**

Deep Breathing Body Scan

Realising he can't fix his worries right now, Ned takes some deep breaths. He relaxes each part of his body in turn, finally focusing on the rise and fall of his tummy with each gentle, deep breath. His mind is soon calm and he falls asleep.
Can you breathe worries away?

Online Only

Sam likes to catch up with his friends online. They chat and play games together, and share funny videos. But even though he talks with his friends, he spends the days alone in his room. He feels restless and lonely.
Why might Sam feel sad?

Fun with Friends

It's great to be in touch online, but now everyone is back at school, it's even better to be together. There are loads more things to do and they plan to meet up at the weekend too. Sam feels really happy. **Do you spend time with your friends?**

I enjoy time with my friends

Bottling Up Emotions

Jay's school project has gone wrong and he wasn't able to finish it. He is really disappointed, and is quiet all the way on the walk home. Dad knows something is wrong, but Jay says he is fine and doesn't want to talk about it.
How does Jay really feel?

Talking Things Through

Dad suggests they make Jay's favourite dinner together. As they cook, Jay tells his dad about his day and finds that sharing how he feels helps him understand and deal with his disappointment. **Can you talk about and share your feelings?**

I can talk about my feelings

Feeling Negative

Maisie is sulking. All of her friends are going away for the holidays. Mum explains they can't afford big holidays, but Maisie still feels left out and thinks her friends' lives are more fun and exciting than hers.
What emotion is Maisie feeling?

Positivity Power

Maisie makes a list of all the things she is thankful for, and she and Mum plan some days out. Maisie realises they can have fun wherever they are, and feels happier now she focuses on the good things in her life.

Can you focus on the positive?

I focus on the good things

 # Worry Wobble

Will hasn't been able to enjoy himself during the summer holidays because he is worrying about starting his new school. He liked his old school because it was familiar and he knew where everything was.
Do you think worrying has helped Will feel less anxious?

Addressing Anxieties

Will shares his worries with his sister and she suggests they look at his new school's website. They find lots of photos and information, and a map too. Will feels reassured and enjoys his holidays.
Can you think of ways to deal with your worries?

I ask for help with my worries

Time on Your Hands

It's the weekend and Ava is bored. She can't think of anything to do, so she teases her little sister, Jasmine, who is painting happily, and they end up arguing. Ava gets in trouble and everyone is upset.

Why does Ava feel so negative?

Valuable Volunteering

Ava is bored, so she asks her dad if they can go and help at his friend's pet rescue centre. They are thankful for her hard work, and she feels happy and fulfilled helping out with the animals and learning to care for them.

Do you help others?

I use my time to help others

Bad Bedtime Habits

Jade thinks sleeping is a waste of time. She likes to stay up late, watching movies and playing games online. When she does go to bed, she doesn't sleep well. She is grumpy and tired at school, and often poorly. **How is staying up late affecting Jade?**

Super Sleep Routine

Jade's mum shows her a video about sleep, and how important it is for good health and well-being. Jade realises she must make changes and starts a new bedtime routine: bath, book, then bed. She sleeps better and feels happier now.
Do you get the sleep you need?

I get enough sleep

Negative Nerves

Tim loves movies and television shows, and dreams of becoming an actor, so when it's time for his school's end-of-year play, he wants to take part. But on the day of the auditions, he is gripped with nerves and afraid to step on stage.

Why does Tim not audition?

Acting Confident

Tim has butterflies in his tummy, but tells himself he is excited, not nervous. He strikes a superhero pose – hands on hips, chest out, chin up – then takes a deep breath. Putting on a big smile, he strides confidently onto the stage.

Can you overcome your nerves?

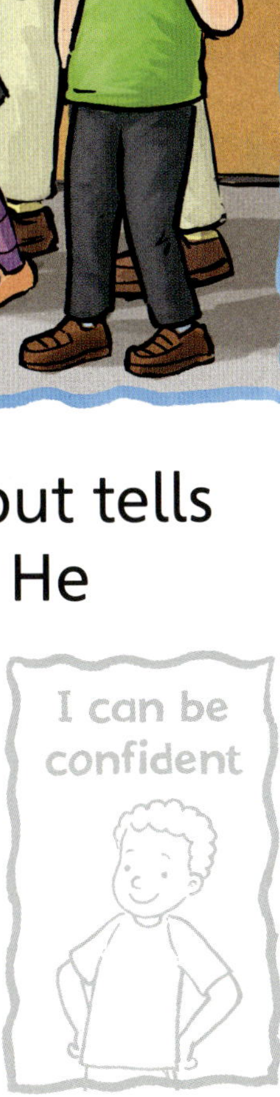

I can be confident

Losing Control

Leo tries to do his maths homework, but he finds it difficult and keeps getting the answers wrong. He gets really angry and pushes his work and pencils off the desk. He is so cross, he can't concentrate at all.
Why does Leo push his things off the desk?

Creating Calm

Dad tells Leo that it's okay to feel angry, but it is better to find ways to manage his emotions and calm himself down. Together, they make a glitter jar. Leo enjoys being creative, and watching the glitter settle makes him feel calmer.
Can you manage your emotions?

I can manage my emotions

Make a Calming Glitter Jar

You Will Need:
- a glass jar with a tight-fitting lid
- glitter
- warm water
- clear glue
- food colouring

TAKE CARE
Dry the outside of the jar before you shake it, as it may be slippery.

How to Make Your Glitter Jar

1. Pour warm water into the jar until it's about half full.

2. Next, add clear glue until the jar is almost full, leaving space at the top for the mixture to move.

3. Now add two or three drops of food colouring and gentlly stir the mixture.

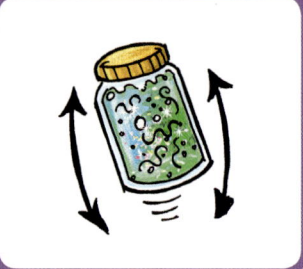

4. Add the glitter. You can use different colours and sizes of glitter to make it really special!

5. Screw the lid on tightly and give the jar a good shake to mix everything together.

6. Now sit and watch as the glitter gently floats down through the jar.

Encourage your child to use the picture stickers and answer the questions in the book.

I focus on the good things

I ask for help with my worries

I focus to keep calm

I enjoy being active

I enjoy time with my friends

I can calm my worries

I celebrate my strengths

I can talk about my feelings

I enjoy family time together

Being outdoors makes me happy

I use my time to help others

I get enough sleep

I can be confident

I can manage my emotions

Use these stickers to show how you feel on the Happiness Diary wallchart, or you can draw in a face instead!

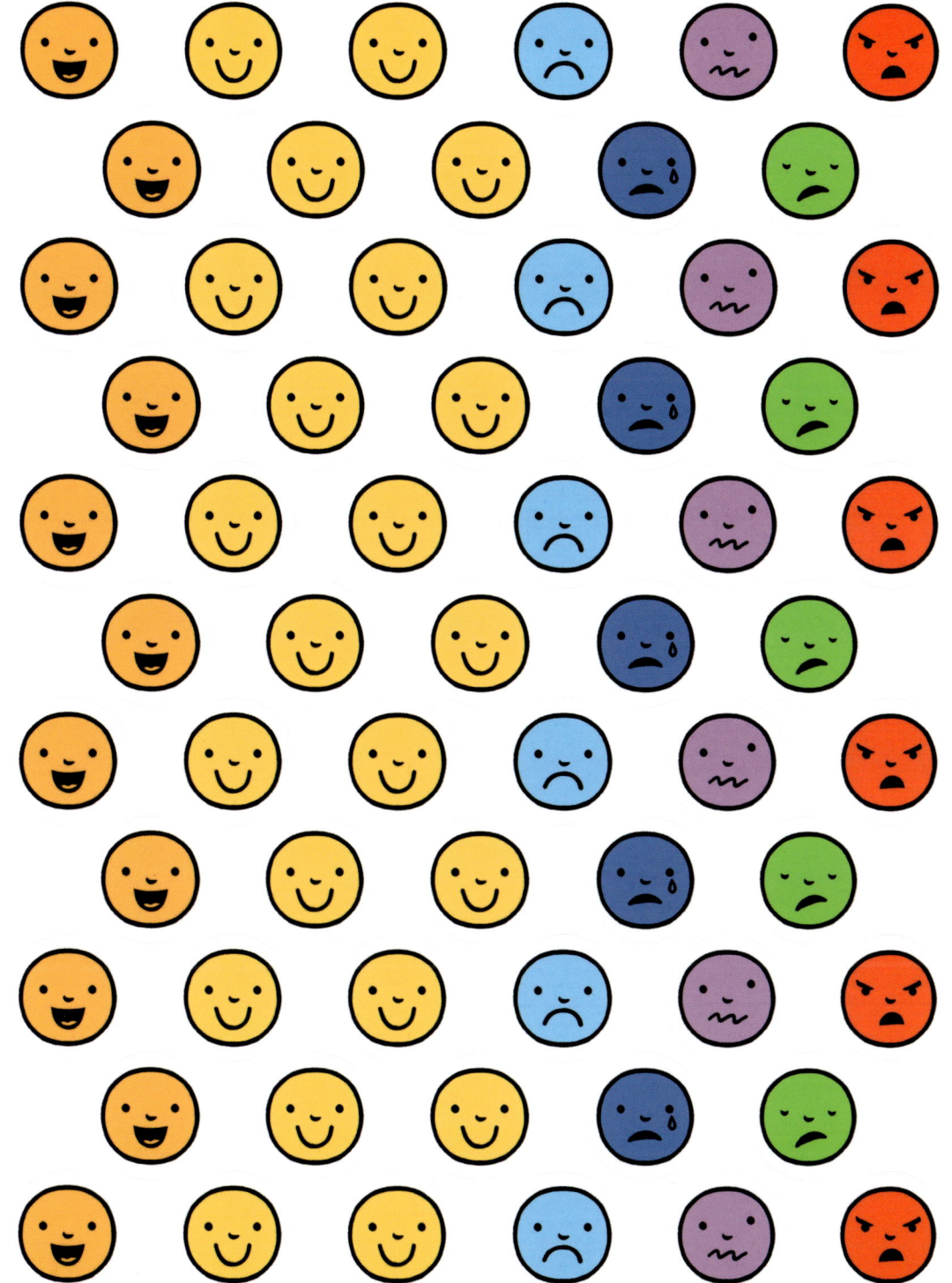